31 REFLECTIONS ON CHRISTIAN VIRTUE

Humility

august, 1997

John,

May these reflections
enrich your journey of faith

Peace,
Bp B L Moreno

31 REFLECTIONS ON CHRISTIAN VIRTUE

Humility

by
Robert F. Morneau

Saint Mary's Press
Christian Brothers Publications
Winona, Minnesota

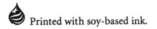 Printed with soy-based ink.

The publishing team included Carl Koch, development editor; Jacqueline M. Captain, manuscript editor; Amy Schlumpf Manion, typesetter; Maurine R. Twait, art director; pre-press, printing, and binding by the graphics division of Saint Mary's Press.

The acknowledgments continue on page 90.

Printed in the United States of America

Printing: 9 8 7 6 5 4 3 2 1

Year: 2005 04 03 02 01 00 99 98 97

ISBN 0-88489-425-8

to the memory of

Bishop John B. Grellinger, DD (1899–1984)—
teacher, pastor, and friend

Contents

Foreword   *8*

Introduction   *19*

1. The Lost Virtue   *28*

2. Things Beyond Us   *30*

3. Humility and God's Will   *32*

4. Comparisonless Humility   *34*

5. As Humble as a Feather   *36*

6. Mary, Filled with Humility   *38*

7. Exalted Humility   *40*

8. Augustine's Late Love   *42*

9. One Mark of Holiness   *44*

10. Song of Humility   *46*

11. Winter Humility   *48*

12. In Praise of Smallness   *50*

13. Self-Knowledge   *52*

14. The Core   *54*

15. Essentials of Virtue   *56*

16. Day of Humble Accounting   *58*

17. Qualities of Worship   *60*

18. Aging   *62*

19. Humility Does Not Diminish   *64*

20. Divine Twins   *66*

21. Christ's Double Humility   *68*

22. Foundation of Prayer   *70*

23. Humility and Service   *72*

24. The Pragmatism of Humility   *74*

25. The Greatness of Humility   *76*

26. A Child in a Green Field   *78*

27. Nothing Belongs to Us   *80*

28. Dear Wormwood   *82*

29. Forgiveness and Humility   *84*

30. This Lowly Thing   *86*

31. God Only Knows   *88*

Foreword

"I was a revolutionary when I was young and all my prayer to God was 'Lord, give me the energy to change the world.'

"As I approached middle age and realized that half my life was gone without my changing a single soul, I changed my prayer to 'Lord, give me the grace to change all those who come in contact with me. Just my family and friends, and I shall be satisfied.'

"Now that I am an old man and my days are numbered, my one prayer is, 'Lord, give me the grace to change myself.' If I had prayed for this right from the start I should not have wasted my life."

(Bayazid)

We have enough evidence that the world needs to change. Each day we witness violence, poverty, hate, and ignorance both close and far. In the face of these realities, we may fall into the same trap as the Sufi mystic Bayazid, directing our attention to all those other people out there who need changing. We may forget the words of Jesus:

"Do not judge, so that you may not be judged. . . . Why do you see the speck in your neighbor's eye, but do not notice the log in your own eye. . . . Take the log out of your own eye, and then you will see clearly to take the speck out of your neighbor's eye."

(Matthew 7:1–5)

Jesus' meaning is clear: we cannot expect virtue—this inner readiness to do moral good—from our neighbor if we do not expect, nurture, and develop it in ourselves. The reverse is also true: the virtue that we nurture, develop, and reflect in our life calls forth virtue in others.

Planting the Seeds of Virtue

We begin to develop virtue where the Sufi mystic's prayers left off, by turning the care of the world over to God and by taking care of our own soul.

To deal with his tendency toward harshness, Vincent de Paul told one of his friends: "I turned to God and earnestly begged him to convert this irritable and forbidding trait of mine. I also asked for a kind and amiable spirit." Vincent's movement of heart toward God involved a surrender to God's presence and power. His prayer also manifested Vincent's need for moral conversion. Vincent knew that living like Christ and clothing himself in Christ's virtues had to begin with knowledge of his own sins and blessings. Times of reflection and prayer, the honest opening and offering of ourselves to God, provide the context for a change of heart, mind, and will to happen.

Reflecting on virtue may be roughly compared to tending a garden. "It was a great delight for me," writes Teresa of Ávila, "to consider my soul as a garden and reflect that the Lord was taking a walk in it." Reflection—the celebration of gratefulness for the goodness in life—invites God to walk in our garden. Reflection welcomes the Master Gardener to plant the seed of virtue within us. Reflection prepares the soil for the seed when it opens our fears, doubts, sins, and goodness to the gaze and grace of the Creator.

The Three Brilliant Flowers: Faith, Hope, and Love

In the garden of the soul, the virtues of faith, hope, and love form the centerpiece. Traditionally called theological virtues, they come as free gifts from God and draw us to God. We cannot earn these virtues; God has already freely planted them in our soul.

However, these virtues need tending. In reflection, we can open our heart, mind, and will to God's grace. We embrace and open ourselves to this grace by pondering and dialoging with God about what we believe, how we hope, and the ways we love. When we ponder the Scriptures and examine our beliefs, we nourish faith. When we meditate on the goodness of God's creation, on friendships, and on all of God's gifts to us, we nourish hope. When we pray for loved ones, consider how we love, empathize with those needing love, and celebrate the love given to us, we nourish love.

A Harvest of Plenty—the Moral Virtues

Faith, hope, and love are further nurtured as we develop the moral virtues of humility, courage, justice, prudence, moderation, temperance, forgiveness, and so on. Saint Augustine and other spiritual teachers maintained that the moral virtues are expressions of faith, hope, and especially love. For instance, in the face of danger to a loved one, people find courage they never dreamed of having. Living prudently—figuring out what is right in a given situation— becomes easier when love reigns in our heart and focuses our will.

Paradoxically, as we develop the moral virtues, we also nourish faith, hope, and love in ourselves. For example, as we grow in justice we begin to look out for the well-being of other people. In short, we grow more loving. Temperance—creating harmony within ourselves—fosters hopefulness.

Growing a Destiny

We change ourselves by changing the small assertions of self, namely our acts, beginning with an act of reflection. The following wise adage—another garden image—provides a helpful way of thinking about this question and about growing in the moral virtues:

> Plant an act; reap a habit.
> Plant a habit; reap a virtue or vice.
> Plant a virtue or vice; reap a character.
> Plant a character; reap a destiny.

Developing our character and destiny begins with the acts that we plant each day, whether consciously or unconsciously. We give shape to our life by each action we take, day by day. A regular pattern of actions becomes a habit. Eventually, our habits determine the shape of our character.

Our character is the combination of our virtues and vices. Our destiny is what finally becomes of us, which depends on the character we build in response to God's grace. A Christlike destiny begins forming with every act of moral virtue. When we pray to be humble, just, temperate, or moderate, when we pray for courage, honesty, and a forgiving spirit, we acknowledge our dependence on God's grace, but we also give our attention to the development of these virtues. Meditating on how these virtues are or are not present in our actions nourishes the seeds of these virtues within us. Reflection on moral virtue is planting, weeding, and watering virtuous acts. The harvest of such reflection will be plentiful: We change the world by changing the small part of it that we are. An old adage says: "Prayer does not change things. Prayer changes people, and people change things." Prayer brings us to the God of love who wants us to live fully, to love, to believe, and to hope. If we open ourselves to God's grace, we will change. Then we can change things.

The God of Weeds

Developing habits of moral virtue takes conscious, consistent effort. The late Robert Hutchins, former president of the University of Chicago, remarked:

> Habits may be lost, corrupted, or diminished. The violin player who stops playing and the tennis champion who stops practicing will soon fall from their lofty eminence. And though the moral virtues are among the most durable of all goods, they, like other habits, may be lost, and for the same reasons.

Like all gardens, the garden of our soul can become tangled and overgrown with weeds, or parched and withered from lack of water. Virtue, like a garden, fails to thrive without attention and care. Reflection tends the garden. It also allows us to ask for forgiveness so that we can start again when we have left the garden untended. The loving God is always waiting to sustain us and draw us back to full life. Our God is the God of Hosea who says about sinful and ungrateful Israel: "'I led them with cords of human kindness, with bands of love. I was to them like those who lift infants to their cheeks. I bent down to them and fed them'" (11:4).

Praying for Virtue

In the Epistle to the Ephesians, Paul tells the community to put on virtue, God's armor:

> Be strong in . . . the strength of [God's] power. . . . Take up the whole armor of God. . . . Fasten the belt of truth around your waist, and put on the breastplate of righteousness. As shoes for your feet put on whatever will make you ready to proclaim the gospel of peace. With all of these, take the shield of faith.
>
> (6:10–16)

To help us clothe ourselves in the armor of virtue, the reflections in this book follow an ancient pattern: listen *(lectio)*, reflect *(meditatio)*, and respond *(oratio)*. Here are some suggestions for using the reflections:

Listen. Each reflection begins with a passage from the word of God, the wisdom of a spiritual writer, or a story. Read the passage attentively at least once, or better yet, several times. Concentrate on one or two sentences that touch your heart; ponder their meaning for you and their effect on you. This type of listening is called *lectio divina,* or "divine studying." The passages are intended to inspire, challenge, or remind you of some essential aspect of the virtue.

Reflect. Once you have listened to wisdom, you are invited to reflect on your own experience. This is *meditatio,* or "paying attention." Each reflection can help you attend to how God has been speaking to you in your past and present experience. If you keep a journal, you may want to write your reflections there. Take the reflection questions with you as you go about your day; ponder them while you drive, wait for an appointment, prepare for bed, or find any moment of quiet.

Respond. Each reflection ends with a prayer of petition and thanks. In *oratio,* we ask God for the help we need in nurturing the virtue. We should never be shy in asking God for help. After all, Jesus tells us many times to seek God's grace, and he assures us that God's help will come. Indeed, the word *prayer* means "to obtain by entreaty." The petitionary prayer reminds us that we are truly dependent on the goodness and love of God for developing the virtue. The response prayer usually gives thanks for the gifts God has showered upon us already. Giving thanks is another way of awakening us to all the wonders of God's love.

Try reading the prayers aloud. They gain a different feel and power. Or use one line as a prayer throughout the day. Plant the prayer line in your heart as you repeat it while having a cup of coffee, washing your hands, or sitting at your desk.

*S*tarting Points

Create a sacred space. Jesus said, "'When you pray, go to your private room, shut yourself in, and so pray to your [God] who is in that secret place, and your [God] who sees all that is done in secret will reward you'" (Matthew 6:6). Solitary reflection and prayer is best done in a place where you can have privacy and silence, both of which can be luxuries in the life of a busy person. If privacy and silence are not possible, create a quiet, safe place within yourself, perhaps while riding to and from work, sitting at the dentist's office, or waiting for someone. Do the best you can, knowing that a loving God is present everywhere.

Move into sacred time. All of time is suffused with God's presence. So remind yourself that God is present as you begin your reflection. If something keeps intruding during your reflection, spend some time talking with God about it. Be flexible, because God's Spirit blows where it will. Gerald May speaks to this when he says:

> The present . . . contains everything that is needed for lovingly beginning the next moment; it seeks only our own willing, responsive presence, just here, just now. . . . There are no exceptions—not in physical pain, not in psychiatric disorder or emotional agony, not in relational strife. . . . Love is too much with us for there to be any exceptions.

Come to reflection with an open mind, heart, and will. Trust that God hears you and wants to support your desire to nourish virtue in your life. Reflection strengthens our will to act. Through reflection, God can touch our will and empower us to live according to what we know is true.

Reflection nourishes the seeds of virtue that are planted in our soul. Listening to wisdom fertilizes the seed. Reflecting on or attending to the virtue waters the seed. Responding with petitionary and thanksgiving prayers shine light on the seed. After the thirty-one days of reflection about humility, you will have planted the seed in rich soil and will likely understand the virtue more fully and have deeper insight into how the virtue plays out in your own life.

God be with you as you reflect on and pray for the virtue of humility and nurture it in your heart, mind, and will. You will be a power for the good of us all.

CARL KOCH
Editor

Introduction

$\mathcal{L}$*ike a Sparrow*

A teacher of philosophy once asked our class to bring in a jar of justice the next time we assembled. No jar was brought. Justice cannot be quantified because it has to do with the quality of relationships.

A teacher of spirituality asked us to define humility. The best the class could do was mention a few images. Humility is more like a sparrow than a peacock; humility resembles a small pond, not the majesty of the ocean; humility might be found in a vigil light rather than the brilliance of a huge stained-glass window.

What is humility? It is that habitual quality whereby we live in the truth of things: the truth that we are creatures and not the Creator; the truth that our life is a composite of good and evil, light and darkness; the truth that in our littleness we have been given extravagant dignity. Monsignor Joseph Gallagher, in his excellent text *How to Survive Being Human,* speaks of humility in these terms: "Humility . . . is the willingness to be what you are and to do what you can." Humility is truth: recognized, accepted, and embraced. Humility is saying a radical yes to the human

condition. Humility is a profound acceptance of God's plan
for us.

God's Word on Humility

Jesus instructed the disciples in the ways of humility.
Indeed, his words turn everything upside down. When his
followers argued on the road as to who was the greatest
among them, Jesus gave this forceful response: "'Whoever
wants to be first must be last of all and servant of all'"
(Mark 9:35). Jesus showed that greatness is not found in
winning the first-place trophy. Rather, fulfilling our duties
in simple and direct ways constitutes humility. Welcoming
a child in God's name will do nicely.

Jesus noticed people scrambling for the best places at
a wedding banquet (Luke 14:7–11). He used this story to
make a resounding statement: "'For all who exalt themselves will be humbled, and those who humble themselves
will be exalted'" (Luke 14:11). Seeking prestige simply
inflates the ego and causes jealousy and division. Envy and
divisiveness thwart the Reign of God. Disciples are called to
build God's Reign. Humility's fruits are peace and a deep
sense of joy, not being first in line.

Jesus humbly embraced our humanity, even death.
In Bethany, while having dinner at Lazarus's house,
"Mary took a pound of costly perfume made of pure nard,

anointed Jesus' feet, and wiped them with her hair. The house was filled with the fragrance of the perfume" (John 12:3). This tender scene foreshadows the anointing of Jesus' body after his death on the cross. Indeed, Jesus reminds the disciples that the perfume had been purchased for this purpose.

As Jesus demonstrated, the ultimate test of humility is how we meet our own death. Only upon our deaths do we know our response to the question, Do you accept the fullness of the human condition or not? Jesus answered yes.

> [Jesus] did not regard equality with God
> as something to be exploited. . . .
> And being found in human form,
> he humbled himself
> and became obedient to the point of death—
> even death on a cross.
>
> (Philippians 2:6–8)

In dying on the cross, Jesus embraced all of us and our humanity. In rising from the dead, Christ exalts us and proves God's saving love for us.

ℐ *Video of Humility*

If a video were made about Christlike humility, this story could well serve as the text:

One afternoon in 1953, reporters and officials gathered at a Chicago railroad station to await the arrival of the 1952 Nobel Peace Prize winner. He stepped off the train—a giant of a man, six-feet-four, with bushy hair and a large mustache.

As cameras flashed, city officials approached him with hands outstretched and began telling him how honored they were to meet him. He thanked them politely and then, looking over their heads, asked if he could be excused for a moment. He walked through the crowd with quick strides until he reached the side of an elderly black woman who was struggling as she tried to carry two large suitcases.

He picked up the bags in his big hands and, smiling, escorted the woman to a bus. As he helped her aboard, he wished her a safe journey. Meanwhile, the crowd tagged along behind him. He turned to them and said, "Sorry to have kept you waiting."

The man was Dr. Albert Schweitzer, the famous missionary-doctor, who had spent his life helping the poorest of the poor in Africa. A member of the reception committee said to one of the reporters, "That's the first time I ever saw a sermon walking."

_A_ Virtue for Our Times

As the story of Albert Schweitzer illustrates, humility confronts an array of contemporary temptations. For starters, consider these five: possessions, pleasures, power, prestige, and perfectionism.

"You are what you have." Possessions have a way of giving us a false identity. Big cars, fancy homes, money hidden away, and wardrobes bulging at the seams with the finest apparel can seduce us to groundless pride. A house fire or a single, major financial crisis throws us back upon ourself in our fundamental poverty. Possessions cannot cover our existential nakedness. Humility keeps reminding us of this basic truth.

"Eat, drink, and be merry." Our culture emphasizes the pleasure principle. We have interpreted the Declaration of Independence in a narrow way: "Life, liberty, and the pursuit of happiness" has become synonymous with individualism and self-gratification. Humility reminds us that happiness cannot be identified with pleasure, but must be broad enough to embrace suffering and sacrifice. Humility accepts pleasure just as it accepts pain and suffering, as opportunities for growth.

"Might is right." Power involves the capacity to bring about or prevent change. Power has its positive and negative sides. When power is used as a means to pursue good ends, we can embrace it. But if power becomes an end in itself, if it is used to exploit and manipulate, then we have entered the culture of death. Humility does not reject power, only its misuse. Humility helps us recognize that all energy and power come from God, and they are to be used to foster a culture of life.

"The best in the west." Success and prestige have become idols. Failure and anonymity are simply unacceptable. Humility transcends this cultural bias and asserts that if prestige comes our way it must be put to the service of God. If our efforts end in failure, we present our poor efforts and good intentions to God, knowing that they are all genuine votive offerings.

"There's the wrong way, and my way." Many of us are tempted to impose our ideas of perfection on others. Refusing to admit our limitations, we throw our weight around, placing exacting demands on other people, running roughshod on those who cannot measure up; that is, we try to play God. The perfectionism that we inflict on others may actually reflect a fear, grown in childhood, that we do not measure up, that we are imperfect. Humility, on the other hand, accepts our limitations and the limitations of other people. In humility, we can open our heart and mind to learn from others. Humility also invites us to forgive ourself and others for failings and to ask God for the grace to see more clearly, love more tenderly, and act more justly.

Humility, Not Humiliation

Humiliation is the opposite of humility. Humiliation implies denying our full dignity as human beings, treating ourself as being worth less than others. Sirach advises:

> Honor yourself with humility,
>   and give yourself the esteem you deserve.
> Who will acquit those who condemn themselves?
>   And who will honor those who dishonor
>   themselves?

(Sirach 10:28–29)

The esteem we deserve is the same all people deserve: no more, no less.

A friend of mine shared a lesson learned early in life. The instruction was his mother's wisdom: There is no one above us, and there is no one below us—we all have equal dignity. A belief that anchors our authentic humility is the faith that we are made in the image and likeness of God;

God said, "'Let us make human beings in our own image'" (Genesis 1:26). We are, as Paul called us, "God's work of art" (Ephesians 2:10). Humility recognizes this truth.

Certainly, we all sin. We make mistakes. We wander from the truth. We struggle with our ineptitudes and incapacities. Humility recognizes this truth, too. Instead of whipping us with these shortcomings, humility turns them into opportunities for grace. Our weaknesses invite us to come before God for help. Humility recognizes that we do not travel alone, but that Christ's Spirit accompanies us as a friend upon whom we can depend. This friend will not humiliate us when we ask for help.

A Pearl of Great Price

The pearl of great price talked about in the Gospels is charity, the grace of love. But a second pearl of great price is humility, the disposition of soul that empowers us to bend our knee before God and to say yes to God's purposes. Although no price tag has been placed on this virtue, we must exercise discipline and prayer to position ourselves to be recipients of this great gift. If we ask in faith, God will give whatever leads to our salvation.

The reflections in this book open a door, giving us brief entrance into how some fellow pilgrims encounter the grace of humility. Perhaps their experience might illumine or challenge our own. It may be that through the sharing of this honeybee virtue, we befriend it and wake up one day to find our feet walking down the humble path of God's love and mercy.

And so we pray:

Gracious God, in Jesus we witness your humility, in your Spirit we know ourselves to be called to humble service. Break our pride, remove our fear, heal us in our blindness. Grant to each of us the grace of humility, so that we might realize the truth of our being and the glory of your majesty. May Mary, humble one, be a guide for us. May Jesus, your child, show us the way. May your Spirit fill us with wisdom that leads us down the path of humility. Grant all this, if it be your will. Amen.

DAY 1

The Lost Virtue

Listen   People who are really humble, who know themselves to be earth or humus—the root from which our word "humble" comes—have about themselves an air of self-containment and self-control. There's no haughtiness, no distance, no sarcasm, no put-downs, no airs of importance or disdain. The ability to deal with both their own limitations and the limitations of others, the recognition that God is in life and that they are not in charge of the universe brings serenity and hope, inner peace and real energy. Humble people walk comfortably in every group. No one is either too beneath them or too above them for their own sense of well-being. They are who they are, people with as much to give as to get, and they know it. And because they're at ease with themselves, they can afford to be open with others.

(Joan Chittister)

■ ■ ■

Reflect   What a delight it is to be in the presence of people who simply are who they are, people who have no need to impress others because they are at home with themselves. More than simple ease, there is truly a graciousness about them because they are graced. No games need be played; no pretense burns up precious energy; no ridicule beats down others in an effort to raise oneself.

Glancing into a mirror, do you recognize any degree of haughtiness, sarcasm, put-downs, airs of importance, disdain? What does the "mirror, mirror on the wall" reflect back to you?

Respond   God, you are present at every moment of my life. You see me for what I am, blessed and limited, gifted and in need of healing. Keep me close to the earth. Empower me to bless you for both my weaknesses and my strengths. May I say yes to your creation, to how I am made. Drive away forever all perfectionism.

Things Beyond Us

Listen In Flannery O'Connor's short story "The Enduring Chill," Asbury Fox comes home to die. His mother insists that he see the local doctor, Dr. Block, much against Asbury's will.

Asbury sat up and thrust his thudding head forward and said, "I didn't send for you. I'm not answering any questions. You're not my doctor. What's wrong with me is way beyond you."

"Most things are beyond me," Block said. "I ain't found anything yet that I thoroughly understood," and he sighed and got up. His eyes seemed to glitter at Asbury as if from a great distance.

Reflect   Most of life is beyond us: the mystery of evil and illness, the origin of the universe and its ultimate destiny, the enigma of birth and death. It is not surprising that we become irritated by not being in control. It is no wonder that anxiety can easily become a way of life. Block, a rural doctor, has got it right. Most of us "ain't found anything yet that [we] thoroughly [understand]." Accepting that fact is the foundation of humility.

Would you agree that the more we know about someone or something simply makes us more aware of what we don't know? Why do we pretend when it is obvious that we are ignorant or afraid?

Respond   Gracious God, without revelation I know nothing of you. Help me understand your love and mercy. Guide me down the path of wisdom and knowledge. Though I will never begin to understand your life in this world, I do have hope for full knowledge of you in the next. Instill in me a humble heart.

Humility and God's Will

Listen   Humility is to be still
under the weathers of God's will.

It is to have no hurt surprise
when morning's ruddy promise dies,

when wind and drought destroy, or sweet
spring rains apostatize in sleet,

or when the mind and month remark
a superfluity of dark.

It is to have no troubled care
for human weathers anywhere.

And yet it is to take the good
with the warm hands of gratitude.

Humility is to have a place
deep in the secret of God's face

where one can know, past all surmise,
that God's great will alone is wise,

where one is loved, where one can trust
a strength not circumscribed by dust.

It is to have a place to hide
when all is hurricane outside.

(Jessica Powers)

Reflect Humble people have a unique relationship with God. They trust God in good weather and in bad. They are grateful for divine blessings as well as for the challenges of life. Humble people know themselves to be loved even in times of drought or menacing hurricanes.

Are you in the midst of any hurricanes or droughts? Call on God. Ask God for protection from the storms and for living water in the drought.

Respond Loving, providential God, send your Spirit of humility into my heart. Empower me to accept my creaturehood, enable me to find my place with you and wisdom in your will. Like Mary, the mother of Jesus, teach me how to say yes to whatever you ask of me. May no sleet or drought, no storm or tempest keep me apart from you.

Comparisonless Humility

 Humility is just as much the opposite of self-abasement as it is of self-exaltation. To be humble is *not to make comparisons.* Secure in its reality, the self is neither better nor worse, bigger nor smaller, than anything else in the universe. It *is*—is nothing, yet at the same time one with everything. It is in this sense that humility is absolute self-effacement.

(Dag Hammarskjöld)

Reflect Dag Hammarskjöld's insight is a piece of wisdom and a cornerstone for humility. If we all have a basic dignity, there is no need to make comparisons. Both self-abasement—put-downs that erode self-esteem—and self-exaltation—the ridiculous attempt to inflate one's ego—become unnecessary when each one of us senses that we possess an innate nobility. Not surprisingly, traditional wisdom informs us that comparisons are odious. Would that more mothers and fathers be mentors in the way of humility.

Talk with God about these questions: Why is our culture so prone to making comparisons? Do you tend more toward self-abasement or self-exaltation?

Respond Gracious and redeeming God, fill me with the joy of self-effacement. May I neither debase myself or others, and may I never exalt myself or overexalt others. Rather, guide me in the way of truth, aware that everyone has an intrinsic worth that deserves my deepest respect.

As Humble as a Feather

Listen   Motionless,
bereft of its wing
and deprived of flight,
imprisoned in a pocket,
weightless as words.

Forgotten,
it surfaces
like a frayed arrow,
some relic of a boy's
lost collection.

And floats,
like the bird,
this slender quill
from the air,
from a thousand journeys.

(Helen Fahrbach)

Reflect Humble things of life: feathers, doorknobs, scatter rugs, ballpoint pens. Things that are there, just being themselves. No acclaim comes their way. No applause. They speak simply of the ordinariness of life and remind us of our creaturehood. Maybe feathers and pebbles are icons of God.

Spend some time today studying birds. Note the intricate designs of their feathers and their flight.

What are some humble artifacts around your house or apartment? What do you learn about yourself by studying humble things like a safety pin, a rubber band, a sunbeam?

Respond *Veni, Creator Spiritus*—come, Holy Spirit, come.
I raise my arms to you.
Carry me on your wings, wise Spirit,
"just like a feather
which has no weight from its own strength
and lets itself be carried by the wind."

(Hildegard of Bingen)

Mary, Filled with Humility

Listen The greatness and nobility of [Mary's] contemplation of God filled her full of reverent fear; and with this she saw herself so small and so humble, so simple and so poor in comparison with her God that this reverent fear filled her with humility. And founded on this, she was filled with grace and with every kind of virtue, and she surpasses all creatures.

(Julian of Norwich)

Reflect One way to understand humility is to position side by side Creator and creature, infinity and the finite, eternity and time. It is both intimidating and humbling to realize the greatness of God's love and our own meager response. Yet it is not humiliating, but rather a source of grace. With this awareness of the way things are, we come into the truth— and this sets us free. Mary's humility made space for grace.

A question: What is the relationship between reverent fear and humility for you?

Another question: When does fear become destructive and paralyzing for you?

And a third question: Do you take time to contemplate, to devote your full gaze toward God?

Respond Mary, queen of all virtue, guide me as I strive to learn the lessons of love and humility. Help me to imitate your simplicity and poverty as pillars of humble life. Assist me in being a person who takes time for contemplation, the prayer that is the pathway to humility.

DAY 7

Exalted Humility

Listen

"Two men went up to the temple to pray, one a Pharisee and the other a tax collector. The Pharisee, standing by himself, was praying thus, 'God, I thank you that I am not like other people: thieves, rogues, adulterers, or even like this tax collector. I fast twice a week; I give a tenth of all my income.' But the tax collector, standing far off, would not even look up to heaven, but was beating his breast and saying, 'God, be merciful to me, a sinner!' I tell you, this man went down to his home justified rather than the other; for all who exalt themselves will be humbled, but all who humble themselves will be exalted."

(Luke 18:10–14)

■ ■ ■

Reflect Coming into God's presence is an awesome thing. Faith would tell us to fall on our knees before the majesty of God. Some of us never learn, protesting that we are better than others. Such self-exaltation is sheer hypocrisy. The tax collector became a model of prayer. Admit to our unworthiness and beg for divine mercy, such is the road to exalted humility. If the tax collector's prayer was the only one we ever said, we could do far worse.

Pray repeatedly the tax collector's prayer: "God, be merciful to me, a sinner!" Ponder the words, letting truth and the feelings evoked sink into your soul.

Respond God of mercy and love, I come before you aware that I am like the rest of humanity: confused, lost, and in need of redemption. I come to you having my limitations and sin. Grant me your mercy and rightness. Send me home in the peace that flows from a humble, contrite, honest heart. "God, be merciful to me, a sinner!"

41

Augustine's Late Love

Listen   Late have I loved Thee, O Beauty so ancient and so new; late have I loved Thee! For behold Thou wert within me, and I outside; and I sought Thee outside and in my unloveliness fell upon those lovely things that Thou hast made. Thou wert with me and I was not with Thee. I was kept from Thee by those things, yet had they not been in Thee, they would not have been at all. Thou didst call and cry to me and break open my deafness: and Thou didst send forth Thy beams and shine upon me and chase away my blindness: Thou didst breathe fragrance upon me, and I drew in my breath and do now pant for Thee: I tasted Thee, and now hunger and thirst for Thee: Thou didst touch me, and I have burned for Thy peace.

(Augustine)

Reflect Humility—the acceptance of truth—leads to confession.
Saint Augustine, a great doctor of the church, admits that
even though God's beauty and goodness were constantly
available and present everywhere, his sick soul lived in
blindness and deafness. Humility led Augustine and can
lead us on a passionate search for God. Augustine longed
and thirsted for God's very being. Even though Augustine's
love came to him late in life, the ancient and new beauty
offered him, and offers us, the grace of peace.

Do you feel an urgency on the faith journey regarding
your call to love and be loved? Do your senses help in your
humble striving to know God?

Respond God of love and beauty, hasten to my aid. The latest whims
easily distract me. My focus on what truly matters vanishes
before mid-morning. Like Augustine, I call to you. Break
open my deafness, shine your light on my blindness, breathe
the fragrance of love upon me. I burn for your peace, "O
Beauty, so ancient and so new."

DAY 9

One Mark of Holiness

Listen   The world which, paradoxically, despite innumerable signs of the denial of God, is nevertheless searching for [God] in unexpected ways and painfully experiencing the need of him—the world is calling for evangelizers to speak to it of a God whom the evangelists themselves should know and be familiar with as if they could see the invisible. The world calls for and expects from us simplicity of life, the spirit of prayer, charity towards all, especially towards the lowly and the poor, obedience and humility, detachment and self-sacrifice. Without this mark of holiness, our word will have difficulty in touching the heart of modern man. It risks being vain and sterile.

(Pope Paul VI)

Reflect Humility is part of a family system. Its brothers and sisters—simplicity, prayer, charity, obedience, detachment,
self-sacrifice—all sit at the same table as the Holy Spirit
sits. All look to the Godward life as the ultimate source of
meaning. Though humility, by necessity, sits in the lowest
place, it gently reminds everyone that what really matters is
to know the ways of God, the ways of holiness.

Which of the markings of holiness—humility,
simplicity, prayer, charity, obedience, detachment, self-
sacrifice—is most important for you at this time in your
life? Does a lack of humility cause sterility in your spiritual
life? Has your humility ever touched someone's heart?

Respond God of all life and holiness, mark me with the sign of the
cross, the symbol of your radical love. May I yearn for the
grace of holiness more than for life itself. Fill my world
with signs of your peace and joy.

DAY 10 ▄▄▄▄▄▄▄▄

Song of Humility

Listen   My being proclaims your greatness,
and my spirit finds joy in you, God my Savior.

For you have looked upon me, your servant, in my lowliness;
all ages to come shall call me blessed.

God, you who are mighty, have done great things for me.
Holy is your name.

Your mercy is from age to age toward those who fear you.

You have shown might with your arm
and confused the proud in their inmost thoughts.

You have deposed the mighty from their thrones
and raised the lowly to high places.

The hungry you have given every good thing
while the rich you have sent away empty.

You have upheld Israel your servant, ever mindful of your
        mercy—

even as you promised our ancestors;
promised Abraham, Sarah, and their descendants forever.

(Psalms Anew)

Reflect Mary, the mother of Jesus, experienced the fulfillment of God's promise of love and mercy. In response she sang her great song of humility and praise—the Magnificat. Mary knew the source of her blessedness; Mary knew that all is gift and comes freely without any merit on our part. Her humility made room for God's entrance into history in the mystery of the Incarnation.

How does your being and your soul magnify God your Savior? Compose your own Magnificat.

Respond God of our ancestors, God of mercy, come to me as you did to Mary, in love and gentleness. Dispose my soul to receive you with joy. Prepare my heart to welcome you as a permanent guest. Remember your mercies of old and teach me to sing, like Mary, of your glories.

Winter Humility

Listen When winter was half over
God sent three angels to the apple-tree
Who said to her
"Be glad, you little rack
Of empty sticks,
Because you have been chosen.

In May you will become
A wave of living sweetness
A nation of white petals
A dynasty of apples."

(Anne Porter)

■ ■ ■

Reflect   Have you ever felt like a winter apple tree, like a rack of empty sticks, shaking in the cold?

In the silence of prayer it is good to remember the angels God has sent into the barren season of our life, those times of awesome humility when we feel naked and abandoned. One of the angels talks of the gift of life, the sweetness thereof that fills us with peace and joy. The second angel loves color and informs us that we are made for glory. We fulfill this call by becoming fully alive. The third angel, the harvester, gathers all our deeds for an accounting. In humility, we ask mercy for the bad, and we give thanks for the good.

Speak with your angels about any winter feelings you are having at present. Ask for help to become even more fully alive.

Respond   God of the heavenly hosts, send forth your messengers that I might become the person you call me to be. Do not let me be discouraged when winter comes to our land. Give me hope and humility that I might recall that I am chosen and destined to be a glad instrument of your beauty and life. Grant me the grace to share my "dynasty of apples" with those in need.

49

In Praise of Smallness

Listen   Of all that God has shown me
I can speak just the smallest word,
Not more than a honeybee
Takes on her foot
From an overspilling jar.

(Mechthild of Magdeburg)

Reflect   Humility points us in two directions. First, it draws our
attention to the majesty of God and the marvels of revelation. Oceans, mountains, the face of an infant, a Bach
cantata: so much God has shown to each one of us. But
there is a second focus in humility's lexicon: human inadequacy. Each revelation demands an entire library, but we
are constrained to speak or write a small word, a faltering
paragraph. We are like a tiny honeybee who stumbles upon
the wealth of an overflowing jar. All the bee can carry
away, in awesome humility, is a tiny speck of glory.

What has God shown you in the last twenty-four
hours? Thank God for any tiny specks of glory that have
attracted you to see God's goodness today.

Respond   God of glory, your brilliance overwhelms my frail sight,
your piercing truth sets my delicate eardrums pounding.
Lead me down the humble path of "enoughness," satisfied
with the smallest crumb of divine food. Do not let me
hesitate to proclaim your goodness despite the inadequacy
of my small speech. Send me a honeybee this day and a jar
of divine jam for my barren table.

DAY 13

Self-Knowledge

Listen   Knowing ourselves is something so important that I wouldn't want any relaxation ever in this regard, however high you may have climbed into the heavens. While we are on this earth nothing is more important to us than humility. So I repeat that it is good, indeed very good, to try to enter first into the room where self-knowledge is dealt with rather than fly off to other rooms. This is the right road, and if we can journey along a safe and level path, why should we want wings to fly? Rather, let's strive to make more progress in self-knowledge, for in my opinion we shall never completely know ourselves if we don't strive to know God. By gazing at His grandeur, we get in touch with our own lowliness; . . . by pondering His humility, we shall see how far we are from being humble.

(Teresa of Ávila)

Reflect Humility is proportionate to our self-knowledge, and our self-knowledge is proportionate to our knowledge of God. Turn this around and the formula is: Ignorance of God fosters pride and self-deception. Time and time again we realize that ignorance is not bliss. Much of our unhappiness stems from being outside reality, from failing to stand in the floodlight of humility that illumines our true self.

Assess the degree of self-knowledge you possess. Ask God to open your heart and mind to the knowledge of yourself that you have particularly avoided.

Respond Humble and gracious God, I live without much vision. Please reveal to me your love and mercy that I might come to understand my true identity. Gift me with humility, the virtue of authentic self-knowledge. Then, in my lowliness, I will ascend to you. Gift me with purity, that I may grow in my knowledge of you. Then, in my poverty, I will be filled with your peace.

DAY 14

The Core

Listen Humility does not consist in hiding our talents and virtues, in thinking ourselves worse and more ordinary than we are, but in possessing a clear knowledge of all that is lacking in us and in not exalting ourselves for that which we have, seeing that God has freely given it [to] us and that, with all His gifts, we are still of infinitely little importance.

(Lacordaire)

■ ■ ■

Reflect Two challenges confront the person who seeks spiritual maturity. The first is clarity regarding our deficiencies. The most brilliant people sometimes are the most humble because they realize that their understanding of life, though perhaps more extensive than that of other people, is extremely limited when compared to the mystery of existence. The second challenge is that maturity is found in those who are keenly aware that all is gift and that nothing can be claimed as ultimately one's own talent or achievement. Such clarity and awareness are products of humility.

What feelings run through you when you think of your gifts and ponder your deficiencies? Talk with Christ about what healthy self-esteem looks like for you.

Respond Generous God, all good gifts come from you. I can claim nothing as my own. In gratitude I praise your goodness and beseech you to grant me the clarity needed to come to clear knowledge of what is lacking in me. Send forth your Spirit of humility to transform my heart and our world. I must not put my talents and virtues under a bushel basket. Rather, may they shine forth and bring you glory and praise.

DAY 15

Essentials of Virtue

 Listen The essential fact about the Christian virtues, what lends them a special savor of their own, is humility—the freely accepted movement toward the bottom. It is through this that the saints resemble Christ. "Who, being in the form of God, thought it not robbery to be equal with God. . . . He humbled himself. . . . Though he were a Son, yet learned he obedience by the things which he suffered."

(Simone Weil)

■ ■ ■

Reflect Humility is not an abstract virtue. It is specific, as specific as Jesus' choice to live a life of simplicity, poverty, and obedience. Most of us struggle in all these areas, seeking to rise to the top, to be number one. Instead of simplicity, we complicate our life by multiple desires and often unattainable goals. Instead of embracing our radical indigence, we seek wealth, power, and prestige. Despite the call to obey God in all ways, we choose to obey our own will, which, in fact, is often a dead end. Jesus, the humble one, witnessed for us the essential facet of Christian virtue—humility.

What are three ways available to you to simplify your life? Ask for the grace you need to take these actions to simplify your life.

Respond Gracious Jesus, by accepting the plan of redemption and by giving up your life for me, you have taught me humility. Strengthen me so that I can follow in your way. Make me a true disciple of the cross. May my humility overflow into joy, the delight of sharing my entire life with you. May I resemble you by my obedience to your word and by my willingness to share your suffering and death.

Day of Humble Accounting

Listen

The wind, one brilliant day, called
to my soul with an aroma of jasmine.

"In return for this jasmine odor,
I'd like all the odor of your roses."

"I have no roses; I have no flowers left now
in my garden. . . . All are dead."

"Then I'll take the waters of the fountains,
and the yellow leaves and the dried-up petals."

The wind left. . . . I wept. I said to my soul,
"What have you done with the garden entrusted to you?"

(Antonio Machado)

■ ■ ■

𝒜eflect Humility involves admission of limitation and failure. None of us can claim a full and adequate response to the goodness of God. Our gardens are not weedless; our gardens at times have become depleted and have nothing to return to the Creator. This fact can lead us beyond humility into shame and guilt. The stewardship question, What have we done with the garden entrusted to us? haunts us day and night. Yet we rely on God's strength to improve our garden, and we hope in divine mercy to transform our failures.

What is the present condition of your garden? How often does your soul dialog with the wind? What return can you make to the Creator for all that has been given to you? Talk with God about these matters.

𝒜espond Heavenly Gardener, I do not walk alone in responding to your call to fullness of life. You continue to energize, strengthen, and forgive me. May the grace of humility help me to be honest in rendering an account of my days. May your grace enlighten me in my desire to bring to you an abundant harvest.

DAY 17

Qualities of Worship

Listen For the life of personal worship—that is to say the increasingly adoring relation to the Holy—is grounded in two qualities: humility and charity. . . . Humility in its beginning arises from negative contrast; man's sense of his own faults and imperfection, his nothingness over against God. But at its height it is caused by positive contrast: the supreme love, worth, and beauty of God in Himself, His perfection striking upon the soul. Charity in its beginning is the creature's response to the divine attraction; and in its fulfillment rises to that unconditioned act of Pure Love which is the very substance of the supernatural life.

(Evelyn Underhill)

Reflect   To find the beginning and the end of anything is a great achievement. Explorers have lost their lives trying to find the fountainheads of the Nile and the Amazon. Spiritual explorers seek to find the starting point of humility and charity. Humility begins in the darkness of our utter poverty and nothingness; it ends, by God's grace, kneeling before the beauty of God. Charity arises out of an acquisitive attraction toward grace; it ends, in God's mercy, in altruistic self-giving.

Are you closer to the beginning or to the end of humility and charity? Who was the first person to get you started on the road of humility? Offer God a hymn of praise.

Respond   I desire to worship you, God of truth and beauty, but I lack sufficient humility and charity. My self-concern blocks my vision of you. My false anxieties distract me from being in your presence. Guide me down the road of love and along the path of humility, so that I come to you and adore you in your supreme majesty.

DAY 18

Aging

Listen Age is truly a time of heroic helplessness. One is confronted by one's own incorrigibility. I am always saying to myself, "Look at you, and after a lifetime of trying." I still have the vices that I have known and struggled with—well it seems like since birth. Many of them are modified, but not much. I can neither order nor command the hubbub of my mind. Or is it my nervous sensibility? This is not the effect of age; age only defines one's boundaries. Life has changed me greatly, it has improved me greatly, but it has also left me practically the same. I cannot spell, I am overcritical, ego-centric and vulnerable. I cannot be simple. In my effort to be clear I become complicated. I know my faults so well that I pay them small heed. They are stronger than I am. They are me.

(Florida Scott-Maxwell)

■ ■ ■

Reflect   Does humility expand or contract as we get older? Doing a
self-assessment, whatever our age, is a great challenge. We
have an innate tendency toward self-preservation, not only
of our body but also of our mind. Our egos are fragile. How
refreshing to see senior citizens candidly list their deficiencies, admitting severe limits, yet not allowing these to para-
lyze them. Humility is the virtue that empowers us to look
at what is, without blinking. It empowers us to embrace our
riches and our limitations.

Are you learning to befriend your faults? If you want
to find out, make a litany of your faults, thank God for
them, and ask God's help in coping with them.

Respond   God of all ages, I come before you in my wealth and poverty. Every good gift is your grace; every fault and fragility
provides an opportunity to turn to you for assistance.
Accept me as I am; transform me in your love. May my
weaknesses also be channels of your grace.

Humility Does Not Diminish

 Do you think I know what I'm doing?
That for one breath or half-breath I belong to myself?
As much as a pen knows what it's writing,
or the ball can guess where it's going next. (P. 16)

Humble living does not diminish. It fills.
Going back to a simpler self gives wisdom.

When a man makes up a story for his child,
he becomes a father and a child
together, listening. (P. 146)

I am so small I can barely be seen.
How can this great love be inside me?

Look at your eyes. They are small,
but they see enormous things. (P. 279)

(Rumi)

■ ■ ■

Reflect Some questions:
- Do you belong to yourself, and do you know what you are doing?
- Does humility diminish or enlarge your life?
- How can such a great love dwell inside your small, humble soul?

Humility contains an enduring paradox. It is such a small seed, and yet it is an enormous tree. Humility displays a radical poverty, yet possesses great wealth. This loneliest of all virtues wears a golden crown.

Respond God, giver of life and breath, may I realize that all is gift and belongs to you. Humble my possessiveness.

God of wisdom and simplicity, you call me to full and abundant life. Tell me the story of gracious salvation.

God of extravagant love, I am little, yet large, in my desire for you. May your enormous, oceanic love flood my being.

Divine Twins

Listen   Equally endearing about this giant of Jewish life [Akiba, a
contemporary of Saint Paul] is his humility. He and Eliezer,
the renowned leader of the academy, were constantly at
odds over their differing interpretations of the law. Once,
during a severe drought, Eliezer was asked to lead the people in prayer to relieve the drought. Nothing happened. A
few days later, Akiba led the prayers; he had hardly begun
when the rains fell. It would have been so easy to smile
smugly or bow his head in false acquiescence as the people
congratulated him, but instead, Akiba turned the event to
his master's favor. He told a story of a king who had two
daughters, one lovable, the other repulsive. When the
lovable daughter came to him with a request, the king
would never grant it immediately, preferring to hear her
voice, to have her with him. The other daughter immediately got what she wanted, so he could be rid of her.

(Paul Wilkes)

Reflect   Humility and humor, if not identical twins, come from the same womb—the womb of God. Their genetic code is essentially the same, composed of truth and a sense of proportion. Maybe God did grant Akiba's prayer just to be rid of him; maybe God loved Eliezer's voice and wanted to hear its faith-filled pleadings. No matter, it rained, and the people did not die.

Have you caught yourself boasting or gloating recently? How did that feel?

When was the last time you had a good, healthy laugh at yourself? Did you share the humor with other people? How did that feel? Ask God for more humor in your life.

Respond   Kind God, listen to my prayers for rain and for peace and joy. Guide me on the path of humility, the road of humor, the way of holiness. Teach me to laugh with myself, with others, with you. In you I find the source of all goodness and life. In you is my hope and salvation.

Christ's Double Humility

Listen You should understand that there are two kinds of humility in Christ as regards his divinity. The first is that he willed to become a human being and so took upon himself that same human nature which had been banished and condemned to the depths of hell. He willed to become one with this nature in the unity of his person, with the result that everyone, whether good or evil, can say, "Christ, the Son of God, is my brother." The other kind of humility as regards Christ's divinity is that he chose a poor maiden and not the daughter of a king to be his mother. Thus it was that that poor maiden became the mother of God, of him who is Lord of heaven and earth and of all creatures. Moreover, of all the works of humility which Christ ever did it can truly be said that God did them.

(John Ruusbroec)

Reflect Our choices reveal our character. Jesus' choices manifest his deep humility. He became one of us, taking upon himself our messy human nature. In God's plan, Mary became mother to the Savior of the world. Nothing glorious here; nothing but a love that reaches out to an enslaved people with the desire to liberate them by love. This love motivates the mystery of the Incarnation, the mystery of divine humility.

Ponder any choices you have made during the past year that reflect the virtue of humility? Then converse with Christ about your humble choices and his Incarnation.

Respond When the Word became flesh, good God, I witnessed once and for all your supreme humility. You took on our human condition; you came to me through Mary, humble and pure. May I revere forever your wisdom and love. May I always choose humility.

DAY 22

Foundation of Prayer

Listen   "Prayer is the raising of one's mind and heart to God or the requesting of good things from God." But when we pray, do we speak from the height of our pride and will, or "out of the depths" of a humble and contrite heart? He who humbles himself will be exalted; *humility* is the foundation of prayer. Only when we humbly acknowledge that "we do not know how to pray as we ought," are we ready to receive freely the gift of prayer. "Man is a beggar before God."

(Catechism of the Catholic Church)

Reflect   Communication with God—prayer—demands humility. Any authentic communication prohibits pride and arrogance, vices that place those in dialog outside of reality. The one thing that makes prayer truly ineffective is falsity. As we enter into our conversation, we are well advised to invoke the Holy Spirit, the Spirit who instills in us humility and crushes the pride that gives birth to the lie.

Call on the Holy Spirit to make you aware of anything you try to hide from God, and ask the Holy Spirit to help you see that you are a beggar before God (though a beggar loved and embraced by God).

Respond   Spirit of wisdom and humility, dwell deep within my heart, so that I might raise up my mind and heart in authentic praise and genuine gratitude. Keep me far from the heights of arrogance. Draw me into the circle of light and fire. I will then burn with ardent fervor and follow more closely the humble path of Christ.

Humility and Service

Listen   For the conduct of the Ashram a code of rules and observances was necessary. A draft was therefore prepared, and friends were invited to express their opinions on it. Amongst the many opinions that were received, that of Sir Gurudas Banerji is still in my memory. He liked the rules, but suggested that humility should be added as one of the observances, as he believed that the younger generation sadly lacked humility. Though I noticed this fault, I feared humility would cease to be humility the moment it became a matter of vow. The true connotation of humility is self-effacement. Self-effacement is *moksha* (salvation), and whilst it cannot, by itself, be an observance, there may be other observances necessary for its attainment. If the acts of an aspirant after *moksha* or a servant have no humility or selflessness about them, there is no longing for *moksha* or service. Service without humility is selfishness and egotism.

(Mohandas K. Gandhi)

Reflect There are many motives behind human activity. Even when we reach out to others in service it might well be that the motivation is basically selfish. In this case, both humility and joy are absent. The grace of humility makes our ministry pure and buoyant. Paul says that "God loves a cheerful giver" (2 Corinthians 9:7). The same holds true for humility. God loves the joyfully humble.

What degree of humility and joy do you bring to your service to others? Would the direct pursuit of humility be dangerous for you?

Respond Jesus, you came to serve, not to be served. Your ministry was marked by humbleness and joy. May my work emulate your zeal. Show me the way of salvation.

The Pragmatism of Humility

Listen   Humility makes it possible for us to be untroubled about our own faults by reminding us of those of others; for why should we be more perfect than anyone else? In the same way, why should the shortcomings of others bother us when we recall our own? Why should we find it strange that others have faults when we ourselves have plenty? Humility makes our hearts gentle toward the perfect and the imperfect: toward the perfect, out of respect; toward the imperfect, out of compassion. Humility helps us to receive afflictions serenely, knowing that we deserve them, and to receive blessings with reverence, knowing that they are undeserved.

(Francis de Sales)

■ ■ ■

Reflect Humility is a pragmatic virtue, that is, it works. It empowers us to be calm in the face of our own and other's imperfections; it gentles our heart by means of respect and compassion; it assists us to receive sufferings and joys in a mature fashion. Imperfection is difficult to embrace; hardness of heart is a perennial danger; exclusion of suffering is a false ideal. Humility connects us to our humanity in a graced way.

Reflect on an incident from your own story when humility worked for you, helping you deal with imperfections and suffering?

Respond Loving Jesus, teach me your way. Help me to look with compassionate love on all my sisters and brothers, and, yes, on myself. Teach me to be gentle and humble of heart, like you, our Good Shepherd. Teach me that no sorrow can separate me from you, no joy is greater than your love. Teach me humility, humility that works to help me be calm in my fear, confident in my insecurity, and loving in my weakness.

DAY 25

The Greatness of Humility

 The disciples came to Jesus and asked, "Who is the greatest in the kingdom of heaven?" He called a child, whom he put among them, and said, "Truly I tell you, unless you change and become like children, you will never enter the kingdom of heaven. Whoever becomes humble like this child is the greatest in the kingdom of heaven. Whoever welcomes one such child in my name welcomes me."

(Matthew 18:1–5)

Reflect Ambition drives us to greatness; humility keeps us within
our appropriate human boundaries. Yet it is well that we
excel in achieving spiritual maturity. A type of greatness
flows from a God-centered yearning, not from some illu-
sory ambition. Jesus gives us a model for such excellence:
the heart of a child. The qualities necessary for participation
in the Reign of God are docility to God's word, openness to
the Spirit's inspiration, a sense of wonder at all God's creation, and a willingness to follow in the steps of Christ. A
true child of God witnesses to these dispositions.

When was the last time you let your child play in
God's creation? Talk with your Creator about honoring and
freeing the child in you to be like the child that Jesus talks
about.

Respond God of all greatness and lowliness, transform my mind and
heart by your grace. I lack docility and obedience to your
will. Instill in me a receptivity and acceptance of your
providential design. Empower me to say yes to your slight-
est request. Fill me with wonder at all you have created.
May I become humble like a child, and may I welcome the
child within me.

A Child in a Green Field

Listen Perhaps the highest moral height which a man can reach, and at the same time the most difficult of achievement, is the willingness to be *nothing* relatively. . . . God makes the glowworm as well as the stars; the light in both is divine. If mine be an earth star to gladden the wayside, I must cultivate humbly and rejoicingly its green earth-glow, and not seek to blanch it to the whiteness of the stars that lie in the fields of blue. For to deny God in my own being is to cease to behold him in any. God and man can meet only by the man's becoming that which God meant him to be. Then he enters into the house of life, which is greater than the house of fame. It is better to be a child in a green field than a knight of many orders in a state ceremonial.

(George MacDonald)

Reflect   When a glowworm sees the brilliance of a star, an impulse toward envy may well emerge. When a star ponders the dim light of a glowworm, there is the possibility of disdain, if not ridicule. An alternative does exist. The worm and the star, the moon and the candle, the flashlight and the blazing lightning might simply embrace their uniqueness and refuse comparison. Among humans this radical acceptance is among our highest moral achievements. It all comes down to obedience, an alignment of our will with God's.

Talk with the Creator of the glowworm and the star about your desire to be a knight when, as a child, you can enter the domain of God; about the degree of light you are asked to share with the world; and about how to cherish the greenness of the grass on your side of the fence.

Respond   God of light and darkness, I long to enter your house of life. Grace me with the gift of acceptance; help me to conform my will to your own. In my marvelous nothingness, I realize that you are the fullness of reality. May your light shine in, and may the glory I radiate bring you praise and honor. Make me a child of your Reign, letting my unique light shine on all.

Nothing Belongs to Us

Listen   Therefore, in the love which is God (cf. 1 John 4:16), I beg
all my brothers—those who preach, pray, work, whether
cleric or lay—to strive to humble themselves in all things
[and] not to take pride in themselves or to delight in themselves or be puffed up interiorly about their good works
and deeds—in fact, about any good thing that God does or
says or sometimes works in them and through them. [This
is] in keeping with what the Lord says: *Yet do not rejoice in
this: that the spirits are subject to you* (Luke 10:20). And we
should be firmly convinced that nothing belongs to us
except [our] vices and sins. Rather we must rejoice when
we would fall *into various trials* (James 1:2) and endure
every sort of anguish of soul and body or ordeals in this
world for the sake of eternal life.

(Francis of Assisi)

Reflect   Saint Francis called his followers to a life of poverty and humility. He had a deep awareness that all is gift, every good thing comes from God. Francis knew that good works and deeds are easily taken home to ourselves, leading to pride and a state of being "puffed up." We can, indeed, take ownership of our vices and sins. Everything else comes from the love and grace of God. Here is where our joy and delight should rest: in the knowledge, by way of praise and thanksgiving, that we are supremely loved. A practical consequence of this is to dedicate our life to God in return for all that we have received.

Ask yourself: Why is Francis, the humble saint who was in love with poverty, so popular in every century? Do I ever become puffed up in the way that Saint Francis talked about?

Respond   God of humility and poverty, help me to live in the truth of things. All life, all holiness come from you. I cannot claim anything, except sin, as ultimately my own. Guide me down the humble path of poverty and love, the only roads that lead to your dwelling. If I stumble, teach me the Resurrection. If I get lost, shine your light of Christ on me. Holy Brother Francis, pray for me.

Dear Wormwood

Listen (An excerpt from a letter written by a senior devil, Screwtape, to his nephew, a junior devil, Wormwood)

My dear Wormwood,
The most alarming thing in your last account of the patient is that he is making none of those confident resolutions which marked his original conversion. No more lavish promises of perpetual virtue. . . . This is very bad.

I see only one thing to do at the moment. Your patient has become humble; have you drawn his attention to the fact? All virtues are less formidable to us once the man is aware that he has them, but this is specially true of humility. Catch him at the moment when he is really poor in spirit and smuggle into his mind the gratifying reflection, "By jove! I'm being humble," and almost immediately pride—pride at his own humility—will appear. If he awakes to the danger and tries to smother this new form of pride, make him proud of his attempt—and so on, through as many stages as you please. But don't try this too long, for fear you awake his sense of humour and proportion, in which case he will merely laugh at you and go to bed.

(C. S. Lewis)

Reflect   Having access to correspondence between devils can be most helpful. It gives us a source for their strategy aimed to confuse us and lead us into darkness. The plan is simple: make us proud of our own humility. The demonic task is to have us focus our attention on ourselves, rather than on God and the well-being of others. The plan is to inhibit self-forgetfulness, a central goal of humility. If these temptations are successful, we will be drawn into the prison of egoism, and eventually to self-contempt. Then Uncle Screwtape will write a congratulatory note to Nephew Wormwood.

Offer God a litany of praise for recent instances of your ineptitude or goofiness. Ask for the grace of a sense of humor and proportion so as to foster authentic humility. Talk with Jesus about situations in which you need a good deal more humor.

Respond   Gracious God, send your angels to me to instruct me. Teach me to laugh at my foibles, to see everything from your perspective, and to embrace life moment by moment. May I be serious (but not too serious) about the journey of faith. May I be responsible (without a messianic complex) regarding my mission in life.

DAY 29

Forgiveness and Humility

Listen

I seek your forgiveness for all the times I talked when I should have listened; got angry when I should have been patient; acted when I should have waited; feared when I should have delighted; scolded when I should have encouraged; criticized when I should have complimented; said no when I should have said yes and said yes when I should have said no. I did not know a whole lot about parenting or how to ask for help. I often tried too hard and wanted and demanded so much, and mistakenly sometimes tried to mold you into my image of what I wanted you to be rather than discovering and nourishing you as you emerged and grew.

(Marian Wright Edelman)

Reflect

Someone once said that confessing one's sins is good for the soul but bad for one's reputation. Humility cares little for reputation. Rather, it has a zeal for the truth, and often the naked truth emerges as we articulate the shadowy side of our life: impatience, negativity, wavering, ignorance, or domineering control. Humility asks for forgiveness and has an intrinsic trust in mercy, human and divine. That is why humility, though innately shy, also witnesses to a noble audacity. The boldness here does not arise out of self-esteem, but from an awareness that we are graced in all we do. A parent's confession—like Edelman's— is especially noteworthy because the passage of time tends to make us defensively righteous.

As a parent or as a child, have you ever made an open confession to family members? What are some things that would ease your soul by seeking forgiveness for them from your family?

Respond Merciful God, I am keenly aware of the extravagance of your love and mercy. Often I have not shared these gifts with others. Rather I have rebuked them and distanced myself because of misunderstanding. Guide me down your humble path. Every night empower me to ask forgiveness and to receive your blessings in gratitude, and fill me every day with your humble love.

This Lowly Thing

Listen

I think I saw it, once or twice,
this lowly thing called humility.
A fellow in the last pew in the city's cathedral,
unable to raise his eyes to the Eucharist.
The elderly farmer, the last load of hay wagoned,
his knees to the ground in thanksgiving.
The midwife, difficult birth done,
whispers to the new mother—"God helped us through."
Humility is so simple,
—eyes lowered, knees bent, thanks given—
yet so difficult for the proud human heart.

Reflect

Sometimes it is difficult to see the intangibles—things such as justice, joy, and humility. But the virtues do become enfleshed in specific and concrete ways, so much so that we can actually see, hear, and even touch them. To do this, however, demands a certain sense and sensibility. We must give up our tendency toward narcissism and turn outward to perceive graces freely offered. Humility is especially difficult to comprehend because of its lowliness. It's close to the ground, somewhat shy, and doesn't believe in trophy cases. In fact, to look directly at it causes severe embarrassment. But it is there, revealing the earthliness of our faith.

Kneeling is an especially good posture from which to both see and experience humility. If you can, kneel down. Ponder your day, and from your knees, thank God for every blessing, even the smallest. Remember that sparrows, not just peacocks, are blessings.

Respond   God of all creation, you have a love for lowly things: sparrows, lilies of the field, small children, the least, and the lost. Help me to foster a similar love. May I treasure your small graces, your little challenges, your humble approaches. Do not allow pride or arrogance to govern my insecure heart. Rather, give me your Spirit of nobleness, your Spirit of radical acceptance of my limitations and weaknesses. May I then manifest your glory.

DAY 31

God Only Knows

Listen It was the common belief in America, Truman wrote, that anyone could become President, and then, when the time was up, go back to being "just anybody again." Recalling his years in the White House, he would say, "I tried never to forget who I was and where I'd come from and where I would go back to." In actual practice, however, it was not so simple. A cartoon in the *Saturday Review* showed a small boy with glasses and a book under his arm, a boy very like Truman had been, walking beside a friend who said, "O.K., so you grow up to be President, and you even get reelected, that's still only eight years. What do you do with the rest of your life?" With his pen, Truman scrawled boldly across the bottom, "God *only* knows!!!"

(David McCullough)

■ ■ ■

Reflect Humility has a good memory. It refuses to forget its origin and its destiny. It is no surprise that humility is a rare virtue because we keep forgetting the basics of life. A president does well to remember a failure at farming. A surgeon does well to recall the early struggles in medical school. A professor is well served by a clear memory of early and recent ignorance. From a spiritual perspective, faith instructs us that our origin and destiny is God. No acquisition of possessions or power can alter that fact. Eventually we all die and face our Creator in humble nakedness.

Ponder these last days of praying for humility. Ask for the grace you need to continue growing in humility. Thank God for graces already given.

Respond Guide me in your ways, gracious God, the ways of humility and truth. How easily I forget that *your* life sustains me every moment of *my* life. Strengthen my memory so that I may recognize my humble beginnings and my humbler end. I will then become a person of praise and thanksgiving.

Acknowledgments *(continued)*

The second scriptural quotation on page 14 is from the New Jerusalem Bible. Copyright © 1985 by Darton, Longman, and Todd, London, and Doubleday, a division of Bantam Doubleday Dell Publishing Group, New York.

Mary's Magnificat, quoted on page 46, is from *Psalms Anew: In Inclusive Language,* compiled by Nancy Schreck and Maureen Leach (Winona, MN: Saint Mary's Press, 1986), page 16. Copyright © 1986 by Saint Mary's Press. All rights reserved.

All other scriptural quotations in this book are from the New Revised Standard Version of the Bible. Copyright © 1989 by the Division of Christian Education of the National Council of the Churches of Christ in the United States of America. All rights reserved.

The excerpt on page 8 by Bayazid is quoted from *The Song of the Bird,* by Anthony de Mello (New York: Image Books, 1982), page 153. Copyright © 1982 by Anthony de Mello, SJ. Used by permission of Doubleday, a division of Bantam Doubleday Dell Publishing Group.

The excerpt on page 9 by Vincent de Paul is from *La Vie du Venerable Serviteur de Dieu Vincent de Paul,* by Louis Abelly (Paris: Florentin Lambert, 1664), pages 177–178.

The excerpt on page 10 by Teresa of Ávila is from *The Book of Her Life,* in *The Collected Works of St. Teresa of Ávila,* translated by Kieran Kavanaugh and Otilio Rodriguez (Washington, DC: ICS Publications, 1976), page 137.

The excerpt on page 13 by Robert Hutchins is from "Make It a Habit," in *Commonweal,* 21 April 1995, pages 14–15.

The excerpt on page 17 is from *The Awakened Heart,* by Gerald May (New York: HarperCollins Publishers, 1991), page 110. Copyright © 1991 by Gerald May.

The excerpt on page 19 by Joseph Gallagher is from *How to Survive Being Human* (formerly published as *The Christian Under Pressure*) (Westminster, MD: Christian Classics, 1988), page 67. Copyright © 1970 by Ave Maria Press.

The excerpt on page 22 is from *More Sower's Seeds: Second Planting,* by Brian Cavanaugh (New York: Paulist Press, 1992), pages 47–48. Copyright © 1992 by Brian Cavanaugh, TOR. Used by permission of Paulist Press.

Titles in the Christian Virtues series

Love by Carl Koch

Faith by Wayne Simsic

Humility by Robert F. Morneau

Courage by Peter Gilmour   Forthcoming

Order from your local bookstore or from
Saint Mary's Press
702 Terrace Heights
Winona, MN 55987-1320
USA
1-800-533-8095

In the garden of the soul, virtues need tending. In reflection, we can open our heart, mind, and will to God's grace. We embrace and open ourselves to this grace by pondering and dialoging with God about what we believe, how we hope, the ways we love, and our desire to grow in moral virtue. When we ponder the Scriptures and examine our beliefs, we nourish faith. When we meditate on the goodness of God's creation, on friendships, and on all of God's gifts to us, we nourish hope. When we pray for loved ones, consider how we love, empathize with those needing love, and celebrate the love given to us, we nourish love.